Fruits

Ann Thomas

CHELSEA
CLUBHOUSE

An Imprint of Chelsea House Publishers
A Haights Cross Communications Company

Philadelphia

Chelsea Clubhouse
1974 Sproul Road, Suite 400
Broomall, PA 19008-0914

The Chelsea House world wide web address is www.chelseahouse.com

Library of Congress Cataloging-in-Publication Data

Thomas, Ann, 1953-
   Fruits / by Ann Thomas.
   p. cm. — (Food)

   Includes index.
   Summary: Presents information on the fruit group of the USDA Food Guide Pyramid, describing various fruits and how they are grown and served.

   ISBN 0-7910-6976-1
   1. Fruit—Juvenile literature. 2. Nutrition—Juvenile literature. [1. Fruit. 2. Nutrition.]
   I. Title. II. Food (Philadelphia, Pa.)
   TX355 .T4515 2003
   641.3'4—dc21

                                    2002000027

First published in 1998 by
MACMILLAN EDUCATION AUSTRALIA PTY LTD
627 Chapel Street, South Yarra, Australia, 3141

Copyright © Ann Thomas 1998
Copyright in photographs © individual photographers as credited

Text design by Polar Design
Cover design by Linda Forss
Illustrations © Anthony Pike

Printed in China

Acknowledgements
Cover: Getty Images

Australian Picture Library, pp. 4 ©T. Bruckbauer, 24; Coo-ee Picture Library, p 19; APL/Corbis, p. 16; Getty Images, pp. 10, 15; Great Southern Stock, pp.12, 14, 20, 23, 25, 21, 26, 27, 29; HORIZON Photos, pp. 15, 17, 28; Photolibrary.com, pp. 6 ©Jenny Mills, 5 ©Trevor Worden, 8 & 9 ©Christel Rosenfeld, 11 ©Jeffery C. Drewitz, 18 ©Robin Smith; Stock Photos/AusChromes, p. 22; U.S. Department of Agriculture (USDA), p. 7.

While every care has been taken to trace and acknowledge copyright, the publisher tenders their apologies for any accidental infringement where copyright has proved untraceable.

Contents

Why Do We Need Food?

We need food to keep us healthy. All living things need food and water to survive.

Horses eat grass and other plants.

There are many kinds of food to eat.
People, animals, and plants need different
types of food.

What Do We Need to Eat?

Foods can be put into groups. Some groups give us **vitamins** or **minerals**. Some groups give us **proteins** or **carbohydrates**. We need these **nutrients** to keep us healthy.

We need to eat a variety of foods.

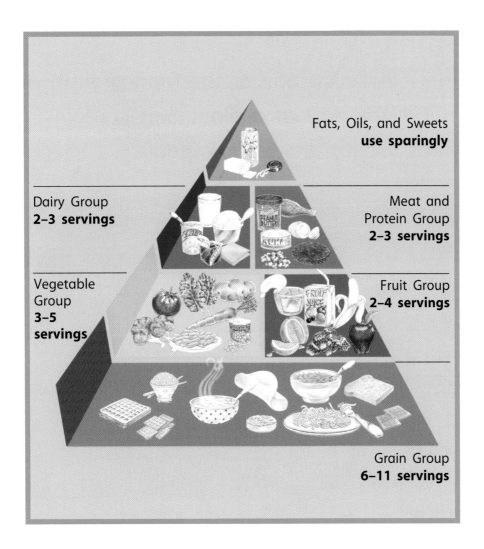

The food guide pyramid shows us the food groups. We should eat the least from groups at the top. We should eat the most from groups at the bottom.

Fruits

Fruits make up one of the food groups. A fruit is the part of a plant that contains seeds. Most fruits taste sweet.

Fruits provide carbohydrates and sugars, which give us energy. Fruits also have vitamins and minerals. These nutrients help us grow and keep us healthy.

Where Fruits Grow

Fruits grow in many places. Apples and oranges grow on trees. Pineapples and raspberries grow on bushes.

Pineapples grow on bushes in hot, rainy areas.

Grapes grow on vines in cooler areas.

Grapes grow on vines that hang.
Watermelons and cantaloupes grow
on vines on the ground.

Fruit Skin

Some fruits have a thick or hard skin. People remove banana and pineapple skins. Apple skin is not as thick. People can eat apples with the skin on or off.

Raspberries have very thin skin and tiny seeds. The seeds are hard to see.

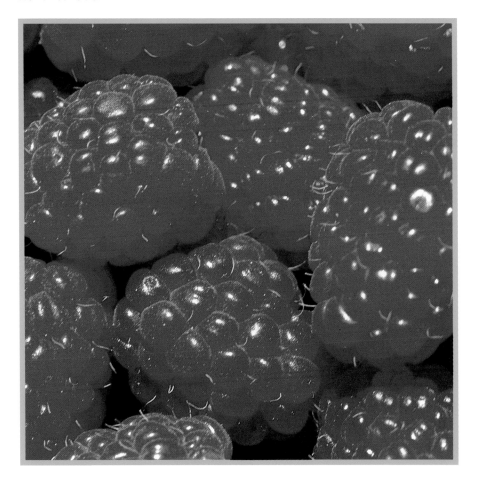

People usually eat the thinner skin on plums, nectarines, and grapes. Some fruits have almost no skin. The skin on strawberries and raspberries is very thin.

Fruit Seeds

Different fruits have different seeds. Apples and pears have several small, brown seeds in the center. Mangoes and avocados have a single large seed inside.

apple

pear

avocado

mango

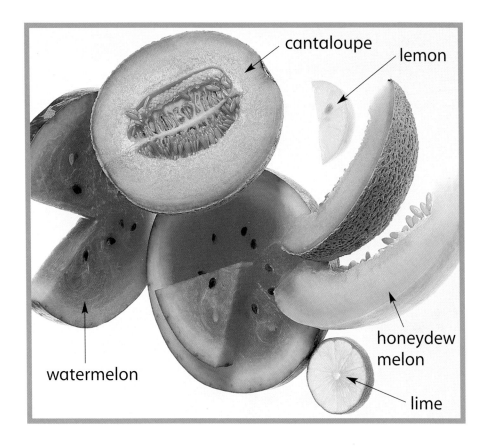

cantaloupe

lemon

honeydew
melon

watermelon

lime

Cantaloupes and watermelons have lots of seeds inside. Lemons, limes, and other citrus fruits have fewer seeds. Strawberries and raspberries have very small seeds on their skins. Peaches, nectarines, and apricots have hard stones inside. They are called stone fruits.

Growing Fruits

Bananas, mangoes, pineapples, and oranges grow best in places that are very warm.

oranges

cherries

Apples, cranberries, cherries, and
blueberries grow best in cooler places.

Farmers grow fruit trees in large **orchards**. They sell their fruits to supermarkets or food **manufacturers**.

Many people grow their own fruits. Some people have their own orchards, gardens, or berry patches. These people sometimes sell their extra fruits at roadside stands or farmer's markets.

Storing Fruits

Some fruits stay fresh longer than others. Apples and oranges can be kept a few weeks. Berries, bananas, and other soft fruits should be eaten within a few days.

prunes   raisins

banana chips   sultanas   orange peel

Almost all fruits can be dried and stored for a long time. Some fruits have a different name once they are dried. Dried grapes are called raisins or sultanas. Dried plums are called prunes.

Raw Fruits

Many fruits are eaten raw. They can be eaten on their own or combined to make a fruit salad. Fruits can also be added to lettuce salads.

Mango fruit tastes good in a lettuce salad.

Most fruits can be squeezed to get the juice. Fruit juice is a healthy drink.

Fruits can be hard or soft. Apples are crisp and crunchy.

passion fruit

Bananas are soft and smooth. Passion fruits are hard on the outside and soft on the inside.

Cooking with Fruit

Fruits can be used for cooking and baking. Rhubarb is a vegetable, but it is often eaten like a fruit. The stems are cooked, and sugar is added to make it sweet. Rhubarb is often made into sauce and pies.

Sugar is added to rhubarb to make it sweet.

Asian sweet and sour dishes sometimes have pineapple.

Tropical fruits such as pineapples or coconuts can be cooked with meats. Some Indian curries are served with mango pickles as a side dish.

Pumpkin is a fruit, but it does not taste sweet. Sometimes it is cooked and eaten as a vegetable. In fall, people often cook pumpkin with sugar and spices and make it into a pie.

Pumpkin pie is often served at Thanksgiving.

Fruits can be added as a topping for desserts. They can be baked in pies, tarts, and cakes. Fruits can be made into jams, preserves, and sauces.

The Fruit Group

We should eat two to four fruit servings each day.

limes   bananas   oranges

pears   grapefruit   blueberries

Glossary

carbohydrate   an element found in certain foods that gives us energy when eaten; bananas, corn, potatoes, rice, and bread are high in carbohydrates.

manufacturer   a company that makes a product, usually in a factory

mineral   an element from earth that is found in certain foods; iron and calcium are minerals; we need small amounts of some minerals to stay healthy.

nutrient   an element in food that living things need to stay healthy; proteins, minerals, and vitamins are nutrients.

orchard   a farm or field where fruit trees are grown

protein   an element found in certain foods that gives us energy when eaten; eggs, meat, cheese, and milk are high in protein.

vitamin   an element found in certain foods; Vitamin C is found in oranges and other foods; we need to eat foods with vitamins to stay healthy.

Index